Dokidokicomics

We are so happy to be a part of your Japanese learning journey,
this book is designed to help you make progress
in your Japanese vocabulary studies.

We hope this book will help you improve your vocabulary skills
and bring you closer to achieving your dreams.

一緒に頑張りましょう！

We are grateful for your support.

Author : Yui Kenmotsu
Illustration : Romain Girard

Contents

Introduction   5

Animals   6

Animals & Water animals   8

Insects   10

Birds   11

Family and People   12

Self introduction   15

Months and Days   16

Time   18

Schedule   20

Social media   21

Season   22

Numbers   26

Money   27

Body parts   28

Organs   30

Face parts   31

Hospital   32

Pharmacy   34

Fashion   36

Buildings and Stores   40

Convenience store   45

City and Position   46

Train   50

Car   53

Transport / Vehicles   54

Airport   56

Drinks   58

Shopping   61

Fruits and Vegetables   62

Dessert   68

Meals   70

Restaurant   73

Sushi	74		Computer	114
Yakitori	77		Punctuation Marks	115
Groceries	78		Stationery	116
Onigiri	83		Colors	119
Kitchen and Cooking	84		Occupation	120
House	88		Sports	122
Cleaning	92		Tools	125
Toilet	95		Hobby	126
Bath	96		Culture	130
Beauty	98		Verbs	134
Nature and Weather	100		Emotions and Feelings	142
Natural resources	104		Opposites	144
Natural disasters	105		Onomatopoeia	148
Space	106		Question	151
Zodiac sign	107		Counters	152
School	108			
Shapes	113			

Introduction

Learning a new language can be an exciting and rewarding experience. Whether you are traveling to Japan, studying Japanese culture, or simply expanding your language skills, this book is designed to help you build your Japanese vocabulary.

 In this book, you will find a comprehensive list of common Japanese words along with their translations into English.
We have organized the vocabulary into different themes such as , food, travel, feelings and more, to make it easy for you to learn and remember.

Please note that to use this book, you will need to know the hiragana and katakana writing systems. If you are not familiar with them, you can find a hiragana and katakana chart at the end of the book.

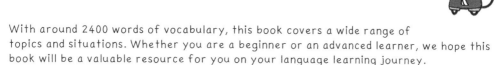

With around 2400 words of vocabulary, this book covers a wide range of topics and situations. Whether you are a beginner or an advanced learner, we hope this book will be a valuable resource for you on your language learning journey.

Animals

ねこ
猫
Cat

いぬ
犬
Dog

うし
牛
Cow

ぶた
豚
Pig

うま
馬
Horse

ひつじ
羊
Sheep

うさぎ
Rabbit

シマウマ
Zebra

パンダ
Panda

くま
熊
Bear

きつね
狐
Fox

カバ
Hippopotamus

しか
鹿
Deer

さる
猿
Monkey

サイ
Rhinoceros

いのしし
猪
Boar

<ruby>山羊<rt>や ぎ</rt></ruby>
Goat

ねずみ
Mouse

<ruby>麒麟<rt>き りん</rt></ruby>
Giraffe

リス
Squirrel

コウモリ
Bat

<ruby>象<rt>ぞう</rt></ruby>
Elephant

<ruby>虎<rt>とら</rt></ruby>
Tiger

コアラ
Koala

<ruby>白熊<rt>しろくま</rt></ruby>
Polar bear

カンガルー
Kangaroo

ロバ
Donkey

<ruby>蛇<rt>へび</rt></ruby>
Snake

ラクダ
Camel

ライオン
Lion

ハムスター
Hamster

あらいぐま
Raccoon

Animals & Water animals

おおかみ
狼
Wolf

たぬき
狸
Raccoon dog

ハリネズミ
Hedgehog

リャマ
Llama

ゴリラ
Gorilla

モグラ
Mole

モルモット
Guinea pig

チーター
Cheetah

ヒョウ
Leopard

ピューマ
Puma

カメ
Turtle

ヤドカリ
Hermit crab

かえる
蛙
Frog

アザラシ
Seal

イルカ
Dolphin

ペンギン
Penguin

さかな
魚
Fish

タコ
Octopus

イカ
Squid

ヒトデ
Starfish

カニ
Crab

クラゲ
Jellyfish

かい
貝
Shellfish

こい
鯉
Carp

ワニ
Crocodile

サメ
Shark

シャチ
Orca

ラッコ
Sea otter

えび
海老
Shrimp

きんぎょ
金魚
Goldfish

クジラ
Whale

ザリガニ
Crayfish

Insects

むし
虫
Insects

あり
蟻
Ant

か
蚊
Mosquito

が
蛾
Moth

はえ
蝿
Fly

カブトムシ
Beetle

バッタ
Grasshopper

ミミズ
Earthworm

サソリ
Scorpion

コオロギ
Cricket

けむし
毛虫
Caterpillar

とんぼ
Dragonfly

はち
蜂
Bee

ちょうちょ
蝶々
Butterfly

むし
てんとう虫
Ladybug

セミ
Cicada

くも
蜘蛛
Spider

ゴキブリ
Cockroach

ほたる
蛍
Firefly

ムカデ
Centipede

10

Birds

とり
鳥
Bird

つる
鶴
Crane

インコ
Parakeet

にわとり
鶏
Chicken

はくちょう
白鳥
Swan

アヒル
Duck

カラス
Crow

ふくろう
Owl

ペリカン
Pelican

キツツキ
Woodpecker

はと
鳩
Pigeon

すずめ
Sparrow

わし
鷲
Eagle

こうのとり
Stork

ツバメ
Swallow

たか
鷹
Hawk

オウム
Parrot

ダチョウ
Ostrich

ハチドリ
Hummingbird

はね
羽
Wings

Family and People

かぞく
家族
Family

ちち
父
Father

はは
母
Mother

りょうしん
両親
Parents

あに
兄
Big brother

あね
姉
Big sister

おとうと
弟
Younger brother

いもうと
妹
Younger sister

そ ふ
祖父
Grandfather

そ ぼ
祖母
Grandmother

おっと
夫
Husband

つ ま
妻
Wife

むすこ
息子
Son

むすめ
娘
Daughter

いとこ
Cousin

まご
孫
Grandchild

おじ
叔父

Uncle

おば
叔母

Aunt

おい
甥

Nephew

めい
姪

Niece

きょうだい
兄弟

Brothers

しまい
姉妹

Sisters

ふうふ
夫婦

Married couple

ふたご
双子

Twins

ひと
人

Person

ひとびと
人々

People

だんせい
男性

Male

じょせい
女性

Female

おとこ　こ
男の子

Boy

おんな　こ
女の子

Girl

あか
赤ちゃん

Baby

こども
子供

Child

おとな
大人
Adult

としょ
お年寄り
Elderly people

にんぷ
妊婦
Pregnant woman

こんやくしゃ
婚約者
Fiance

ともだち
友達
Friend

しんゆう
親友
Best friend

どうりょう
同僚
Colleague

どくしん
独身
Single

かれし
彼氏
Boyfriend

かのじょ
彼女
Girlfriend

りんじん
隣人
Neighbor

クラスメイト
Classmates

わかもの
若者
Young people

しんたいしょうがいしゃ
身体障害者
Person with disabilities

みんぞく
民族
Ethnic group

りこんしゃ
離婚者
Divorced person

Self introduction

じ こ しょうかい
自己紹介
Self-introduction

プロフィール
Profile

な まえ
名前
Name

せいねんがっぴ
生年月日
Date of birth

じゅう しょ
住所
Address

でん わ ばんごう
電話番号
Telephone number

メールアドレス
E-mail address

しょくぎょう
職業
Profession

こくせき
国籍
Nationality

しゅ み
趣味
Hobby

けつ えき がた
血液型
Blood type

せい ざ
星座
Zodiac sign

せい べつ
性別
Gender

ねんれい
年齢
Age

しょめい
署名
Signature

がくれき
学歴
Educational
background

15

Months and Days

いち がつ
一 月
January

に がつ
二 月
February

さん がつ
三 月
March

し がつ
四 月
April

ご がつ
五 月
May

ろく がつ
六 月
June

しち がつ
七 月
July

はち がつ
八 月
August

く がつ
九 月
September

じゅうがつ
十 月
October

じゅういちがつ
十 一 月
November

じゅうにがつ
十 二 月
December

ようび
曜 日
Day of the week

げつようび
月 曜 日
Monday

か ようび
火 曜 日
Tuesday

すい ようび
水 曜 日
Wednesday

もくようび
木 曜 日
Thursday

きん ようび
金 曜 日
Friday

ど ようび
土 曜 日
Saturday

にち ようび
日 曜 日
Sunday

ついたち
一日
1st

ふつか
二日
2nd

みっか
三日
3rd

よっか
四日
4th

いつか
五日
5th

むいか
六日
6th

なのか
七日
7th

ようか
八日
8th

ここのか
九日
9th

とおか
十日
10th

じゅういちにち
十一日
11th

じゅうににち
十二日
12th

じゅうさんにち
十三日
13th

じゅうよっか
十四日
14th

じゅうごにち
十五日
15th

じゅうろくにち
十六日
16th

じゅうななにち
十七日
17th

じゅうはちにち
十八日
18th

じゅうくにち
十九日
19th

はつか
二十日
20th

Time

じ かん
時 間
Time

じ
時
Hour

ふん / ぶん
分
Minute

びょう
秒
Second

あさ
朝
Morning

ひる
昼
Noon

ゆうがた
夕方
Afternoon

よる
夜
Night

ご ぜん
午前
During morning

ご ご
午後
During afternoon

ひ / にち
日
Day

しゅう
週
Week

つき
月
Month

ねん
年
Year

しゅうまつ
週 末
Weekend

ねんまつ
年 末
The end of the year

おととい

一昨日

Before yesterday

きのう

昨日

Yesterday

きょう

今日

Today

あした

明日

Tomorrow

あさって

明後日

Day after tomorrow

せんせんしゅう

先々週

The week before last

せんしゅう

先週

Last week

こんしゅう

今週

This week

らいしゅう

来週

Next week

さらいしゅう

再来週

The week after next

おととし

一昨年

The year before last

きょねん

去年

Last year

ことし

今年

This year

らいねん

来年

Next year

さらいねん

再来年

The year after next

カレンダー

Calendar

Schedule

てちょう
手帳
Schedule planner

ひづけ
日付
Date

にっき
日記
Journal

しごと
仕事
Work

がっこう
学校
School

たんじょうび
誕生日
Birthday

デート
Go on a date

けっこんきねんび
結婚記念日
Wedding anniversary

よてい
予定
Plan

もくひょう
目標
Goal

りょこう
旅行
Travel

か　もの
買い物
Shopping

きゅうりょうび
給料日
Payday

パーティー
Party

かいぎ
会議
Meeting

なら　ごと
習い事
Take lesson

Social media

エスエヌエス
SNS
Social media

いいね
Like

ハッシュタグ
Hashtag

コメント
Comment

プロフィール
Profile

メッセージ
Message

シェア
Share

とうこう
投稿する
Post

バズる
Go viral

フォロワー
Follower

コミュニティー
Community

ライブ
Live

つうち
通知
Notification

えんじょう
炎上
Blow up

ともだち
友達
Friends

ほぞん
保存する
Save

Season

<ruby>季節<rt>き せつ</rt></ruby>

Seasons

<ruby>春<rt>はる</rt></ruby>

Spring

<ruby>ひ な 祭 り<rt>まつ</rt></ruby>

Doll festival

ホワイトデー

White day

<ruby>卒 業 式<rt>そつぎょうしき</rt></ruby>

Graduation ceremony

<ruby>春 分 の 日<rt>しゅんぶん   ひ</rt></ruby>

Spring Equinox Day

<ruby>桜<rt>さくら</rt></ruby>

Cherry blossoms

<ruby>花 見<rt>はな み</rt></ruby>

Cherry-blossom viewing

<ruby>入 学 式<rt>にゅう がく しき</rt></ruby>

School entrance ceremony

<ruby>鯉 の ぼ り<rt>こい</rt></ruby>

Carp streamer

<ruby>子 供 の 日<rt>こ ども   ひ</rt></ruby>

Children's Day

<ruby>母 の 日<rt>はは   ひ</rt></ruby>

Mother's Day

<ruby>筍<rt>たけのこ</rt></ruby>

Bamboo shoot

<ruby>苺 狩 り<rt>いちご が</rt></ruby>

Strawberry picking

<ruby>桜 餅<rt>さくら もち</rt></ruby>

Sakura mochi

<ruby>花 粉<rt>か ふん</rt></ruby>

Pollen

なつ
夏
Summer

つ ゆ
梅 雨
Rainy season

ち ち ひ
父 の 日
Father's Day

たなばた
七 夕
Star festival

うみ ひ
海 の 日
Marine Day

ぼん
お 盆
Obon holiday

なつ やす
夏 休 み
Summer vacations

はな び たい かい
花 火 大 会
Firework festival

なつ まつ
夏 祭 り
Summer festival

ご おり
か き 氷
Shaved ice

ゆかた
浴 衣
Yukata

ひまわり
Sunflower

キャンプ
Camp

あさがお
Morning glory

わ
スイカ割り
Watermelon smashing

うちわ
Paper fan

あき
秋
Autumn

けいろう ひ
敬老の日
Respect for the
Aged Day

しゅうぶん ひ
秋分の日
Autumnal Equinox
Day

つきみ
月見
Moon viewing

たいいく ひ
体育の日
Health and Sports
day

ハロウィン
Halloween

かぼちゃ
Pumpkin

や いも
焼き芋
Roasted sweet potato

ぶん か ひ
文化の日
Culture Day

しちごさん
七五三
Festival for the
children aged 3, 5, 7
years old

こうよう
紅葉
Autumn leaves

きんろうかんしゃ ひ
勤労感謝の日
Labor Thanksgiving
Day

イチョウ
Ginkgo

くり
栗
Chestnut

きのこ
Mushrooms

ハイキング
Hiking

ふゆ
冬
Winter

イルミネーション
Illumination

ゆき
雪だるま
Snowman

ゆきまつ
雪祭り
Snow festival

クリスマス
Christmas

ぼうねんかい
忘年会
Year-end party

おおみそか
大晦日
New Year's Eve

としこ
年越しそば
Soba noodles eaten
on New year eve

がんたん
元旦
New Year

もち
餅つき
Pounding mochi

おせち
Japanese Traditional
New Year's dish

せいじん　ひ
成人の日
Coming of Age day

バレンタイン
Saint-valentin

おんせん
温泉
Hot spring

おに
鬼
Oni (Devil)

せつぶん
節分
Setsubun,
on the day we throw
away beans with
saying
(Devils out Happiness
in)

Numbers

いち
一
One

に
二
Two

さん
三
Three

し / よん
四
Four

ご
五
Five

ろく
六
Six

しち / なな
七
Seven

はち
八
Eight

きゅう
九
Nine

じゅう
十
Ten

にじゅう
二十
Twenty

さんじゅう
三十
Thirty

よんじゅう
四十
Fourty

ごじゅう
五十
Fifty

ろくじゅう
六十
Sixty

ななじゅう
七十
Seventy

はちじゅう
八十
Eighty

きゅうじゅう
九十
Ninety

ひゃく
百
Hundred

せん
千
Thousand

Money

かね
お金
Money

えん
円
Yen

いち えん
一円
1 yen

ご えん
五円
5 yen

じゅう えん
十円
10 yen

ご じゅう えん
五十円
50 yen

ひゃく えん
百円
100 yen

ご ひゃく えん
五百円
500 yen

せん えん
千円
1000 yen

に せん えん
二千円
2000 yen

ご せん えん
五千円
5000 yen

いち まん えん
一万円
10,000 yen

じゅう まん えん
十万円
100,000 yen

ひゃく まん えん
百万円
Millions yen

いっ せん まん えん
一千万円
10 million yen

いち おく えん
一億円
100 million yen

いっ ちょう えん
一兆円
1 trillion yen

つう か
通貨
Currency

かね も
お金持ち
Rich

びん ぼう
貧乏
Poor

Body parts

くび
首
Neck

かた
肩
Shoulder

うで
腕
Arm

わき
わき
Armpit

のど
喉
Throat

ひじ
肘
Elbow

て
手
Hand

てくび
手首
Wrist

ゆび
指
Finger

むね
胸
Chest

ちぶさ
乳房
Breast

なか
お腹
Belly

へそ
Belly button

こし
腰
Lower back

せなか
背中
Back

つめ
爪
Nail

しり
お尻
Bottom

あし
脚
Legs

ひざ
膝
Knees

ふと
太もも
Thighs

<ruby>足<rt>あし</rt></ruby>

Foot

<ruby>足<rt>あし</rt></ruby> <ruby>首<rt>くび</rt></ruby>

Ankle

ふくらはぎ

Calves

かかと

Heel

<ruby>足<rt>あし</rt></ruby> の <ruby>指<rt>ゆび</rt></ruby>

Toe

<ruby>足<rt>あし</rt></ruby> の <ruby>甲<rt>こう</rt></ruby>

Instep

<ruby>体<rt>からだ</rt></ruby>

Body

<ruby>親<rt>おや</rt></ruby><ruby>指<rt>ゆび</rt></ruby>

Thumb

<ruby>人<rt>ひと</rt></ruby><ruby>差<rt>さ</rt></ruby>し <ruby>指<rt>ゆび</rt></ruby>

Index finger

<ruby>中<rt>なか</rt></ruby><ruby>指<rt>ゆび</rt></ruby>

Middle finger

<ruby>薬<rt>くすり</rt></ruby><ruby>指<rt>ゆび</rt></ruby>

Ring finger

<ruby>小<rt>こ</rt></ruby><ruby>指<rt>ゆび</rt></ruby>

Pinky

<ruby>肌<rt>はだ</rt></ruby>

Skin

<ruby>筋<rt>きん</rt></ruby><ruby>肉<rt>にく</rt></ruby>

Muscle

<ruby>骨<rt>ほね</rt></ruby>

Bone

<ruby>脊<rt>せき</rt></ruby><ruby>髄<rt>ずい</rt></ruby>

Spinal cord

<ruby>肋<rt>ろっ</rt></ruby><ruby>骨<rt>こつ</rt></ruby>

Rib

<ruby>頭<rt>ず</rt></ruby><ruby>蓋<rt>がい</rt></ruby><ruby>骨<rt>こつ</rt></ruby>

Skull

<ruby>背<rt>せ</rt></ruby><ruby>骨<rt>ぼね</rt></ruby>

Backbone

<ruby>骨<rt>こつ</rt></ruby><ruby>盤<rt>ばん</rt></ruby>

Pelvis

Organs

ない ぞう
内 臓

Internal organs

しん ぞう
心 臓

Heart

もう さい けっ かん
毛 細 血 管

Capillaries

い
胃

Stomach

はい
肺

Lung

しょく どう
食 道

Esophagus

かん ぞう
肝 臓

Liver

のう
脳

Brain

けっ かん
血 管

Blood vessel

じん ぞう
腎 臓

Kidney

ぞう
すい 臓

Pancreas

ひ ぞう
脾 臓

Spleen

だい ちょう
大 腸

Large intestine

しょう ちょう
小 腸

Small intestine

にょう どう
尿 道

Urethra

ぼう こう
膀 胱

Bladder

Face parts

かお
顔
Face

かみ
髪
Hair

まゆげ
眉毛
Eyebrows

め
目
Eyes

おでこ
Forehead

あたま
頭
Head

みみ
耳
Ears

はな
鼻
Nose

ほお
頬
Cheeks

げ
まつ毛
Eyelashes

まぶた
Eyelids

くち
口
Mouth

くちびる
唇
Lips

は
歯
Teeth

した
舌
Tongue

あご
顎
Chin / Jaw

ひげ
髭
Beard

ほくろ
Beauty spot

くま
隈
Bags under eyes

ニキビ
Acne

Hospital

びょういん
病院
Hospital

いしゃ
医者
Doctor

かんごし
看護師
Nurse

かんじゃ
患者
Patient

ほけんしょう
保険証
Insurance card

しんさつけん
診察券
Patient registration card

もんしんひょう
問診票
Medical questionnaire

しんさつしつ
診察室
Consulting room

てんてき
点滴
I.V.

しゅじゅつ
手術
Surgery

にゅういん
入院
Hospitalization

たいいん
退院
Hospital discharge

たいおんけい
体温計
Thermometer

ちゅうしゃ
注射
Injection

ほうたい
包帯
Bandage

ち
血
Blood

レントゲン

Xray

いがく
医学

Medical science

ますい
麻酔

Anesthesia

めまい

Dizzy

けつえきけんさ
血液検査

Blood test

たいじゅうそくてい
体重測定

Weight measurement

びょうき
病気

Illness

きんにくつう
筋肉痛

Muscle pain

こっせつ
骨折

Fracture

ふくさよう
副作用

Side effect

まつばづえ
松葉杖

Crutch

くるまいす
車椅子

Wheelchair

しょくちゅうどく
食中毒

Food poisoning

けが
怪我

Injury

インフルエンザ

Flu

ワクチン

Vaccine

Pharmacy

やっきょく
薬局
Pharmacy

やくざいし
薬剤師
Pharmacist

しょほうせん
処方箋
Prescription

くすり
薬
Medicine

じょうざい
錠剤
Tablet

アレルギー
Allergy

かぜ
風邪
Cold

ねつ
熱
Fever

せき
咳
Cough

きず
傷
Wound

やけど
火傷
Burn

はなみず
鼻水
Runny nose

いた
痛み
Pain

くしゃみ
Sneezing

ずつう
頭痛
Headache

ふくつう
腹痛
Stomachache

<ruby>目<rt>め</rt></ruby><ruby>薬<rt>ぐすり</rt></ruby>

Eye drop

<ruby>痛<rt>いた</rt></ruby>み<ruby>止<rt>ど</rt></ruby>め

Painkiller

<ruby>痒<rt>かゆ</rt></ruby>み<ruby>止<rt>ど</rt></ruby>め

Anti-itch medicine

<ruby>風邪薬<rt>かぜぐすり</rt></ruby>

Cold medicine

<ruby>湿布<rt>しっぷ</rt></ruby>

Cold compress

<ruby>薬用<rt>やくよう</rt></ruby>シロップ

Medical syrup

<ruby>塗<rt>ぬ</rt></ruby>り<ruby>薬<rt>ぐすり</rt></ruby>

Ointment

<ruby>粉薬<rt>こなぐすり</rt></ruby>

Powder medicine

マスク

Mask

<ruby>絆創膏<rt>ばんそうこう</rt></ruby>

Band-aid

ティッシュ

Tissue

コンタクト<ruby>用品<rt>ようひん</rt></ruby>

Contact lens
care products

<ruby>生理用品<rt>せいりようひん</rt></ruby>

Sanitary products

<ruby>紙<rt>かみ</rt></ruby>おむつ

Diaper

サプリメント

Supplement

ウエットティッシュ

Wet wipes

Fashion

ふく
服
Clothes

ジャケット
Jacket

シャツ
Shirt

ワンピース
Dress

スカート
Skirt

ズボン
Pants

スーツ
Suit

コート
Coat

ジーパン
Jeans

カーディガン
Cardigan

トレーナー
Sweatshirt

パーカー
Hoodie

ティーシャツ
T-shirt

ロンティー
Long T-shirt

セーター
Sweater

たん
短パン
Shorts

36

ブラウス
Blouse

ドレス
Dress

かわ
革ジャン
Leather jacket

タートルネック
Turtleneck

ミニスカート
Miniskirt

ポロシャツ
Polo shirt

パジャマ
Pajamas

レインコート
Raincoat

ブーツ
Boots

サンダル
Sandals

ヒール
Heels

なが ぐつ
長靴
Rain boots

スニーカー
Sneakers

ビーチサンダル
Flip Flops

くつ
靴
Shoes

スリッパ
Slippers

ネクタイ
Tie

かばん
鞄
Bag

ぼうし
帽子
Hat

スカーフ
Scarf

マフラー
Winter scarf

ベルト
Belt

こぜにいれ
小銭入れ
Change purse

かさ
傘
Umbrella

うでどけい
腕時計
Watch

ゆびわ
指輪
Ring

ネックレス
Necklace

みずぎ
水着
Swimsuit

めがね
Glasses

リュックサック
Backpack

さいふ
財布
Wallet

サングラス
Sunglasses

したぎ
下着
Underwear

トランクス
Boxers

くつした
靴下
Socks

てぶくろ
手袋
Gloves

むぎ　　ぼうし
麦わら帽子
Straw hat

みみ
耳あて
Ear muffs

キャップ
Cap

ぼう
ニット帽
Beanie

めん
綿
Cotton

ウール
Wool

かわ
革
Leather

あさ
麻
Hemp

そで
袖
Sleeve

えり
襟
Collar

ポケット
Pocket

ボタン
Buttons

39

Buildings and Stores

たて もの
建物
Buildings

しゃくしょ
市役所
City Hall

けいさつしょ
警察署
Police Station

こうばん
交番
Police box

しょうぼうしょ
消防署
Fire station

たいしかん
大使館
Embassy

りょうじかん
領事館
Consulate

さいばんしょ
裁判所
Courthouse

きょうかい
教会
Church

けいむしょ
刑務所
Prison

こうじょう
工場
Factory

ガソリンスタンド
Gas station

びょういん
美容院
Hair salon

しかいいん
歯科医院
Dental clinic

としょかん
図書館
Library

えいがかん
映画館
Movie theater

びじゅつかん
美術館
Art museum

どうぶつえん
動物園
Zoo

すいぞくかん
水族館
Aquarium

はくぶつかん
博物館
Museum

ゆうえんち
遊園地
Amusement park

ホテル
Hotel

りょかん
旅館
Japanese style hotel

せんとう
銭湯
Public bath

てら
寺
Temple

じんじゃ
神社
Shinto Shrine

しろ
城
Castle

みせ
店
Store

コンビニ
Convenience store

レストラン
Restaurant

コインランドリー
Laundromat

クリーニング屋
や
Dry cleaner

びょういん
病院
Hospital

やっきょく
薬局
Pharmacy

ゆうびん きょく
郵便局
Post office

ぎんこう
銀行
Bank

いえ
家
House

アパート
2 story apartment

マンション
Apartment with more
than 3 floors

がっこう
学校
School

くうこう
空港
Airport

えき
駅
Train station

スタジアム
Stadium

しょうてんがい
商店街
Shopping arcade

そうこ
倉庫
Warehouse

げきじょう
劇場
Theater

いちば
市場
Market

ペットショップ
Pet shop

<ruby>パ<rt>や</rt></ruby>
パン屋

Bakery

花屋

Flower shop

スーパー

Supermarket

本屋

Bookstore

魚屋

Fish market

肉屋

Butcher

八百屋

Greengrocer

ケーキ屋

Cake shop

喫茶店

Coffee shop

文房具屋

Stationery shop

靴屋

Shoe shop

服屋

Clothing store

ラーメン屋

Ramen restaurant

寿司屋

Sushi restaurant

居酒屋

Izakaya (Japanese bar)

百貨店

Department store

ふどうさん や
不動産屋
Real estate agency

えん
100円ショップ
100 yen shop

さか や
酒屋
Liquor store

リサイクルショップ
Secondhand shop

じ てん しゃ や
自転車屋
Bicycle shop

めがね や
眼鏡屋
Eyeglass store

けい たい でん わ や
携帯電話屋
Cell phone store

と けい や
時計屋
Watch store

しゅげい ようひん てん
手芸用品店
Handcrafts store

わ が し や
和菓子屋
Japanese sweets
shop

おもちゃ屋
Toy shop

しゅう り や
修理屋
Repair shop

か でん りょう はん てん
家電量販店
Electronic and home
appliances store

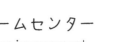
ホームセンター
Home improvement
store

や たい
屋台
Food stall

ショッピングセンター
Mall

44

Convenience store

コンビニ
Convenience store

ATM
ATM

コピー機
き
Copy machine

新聞
しんぶん
Newspaper

雑誌
ざっし
Magazine

カップ麺
めん
Cup noodle

弁当
べんとう
Boxed lunch

菓子パン
かし
Sweet bread

缶ジュース
かん
Canned juice

お茶
ちゃ
Green tea

コロッケ
Croquette

唐揚げ
からあ
Japanese fried chicken

コーヒー
Coffee

Sサイズ
エス
Small size

Mサイズ
エム
Medium size

Lサイズ
エル
Large size

お握り
にぎ
Rice ball

サンドイッチ
Sandwich

肉まん
にく
Steamed pork bun

アイス
Ice cream

City and Position

どうろ
道路
Road

おうだんほどう
横断歩道
Crosswalk

こうそくどうろ
高速道路
Highway

はし
橋
Bridge

しんごう
信号
Traffic signal

ふみきり
踏切
Railroad crossing

じどうはんばいき
自動販売機
Vending machine

ゆうびん
郵便ポスト
Post box

てい
バス停
Bus stop

のば
タクシー乗り場
Cab stand

こうさてん
交差点
Intersection

ひょうしき
標識
Sign

ほどう
歩道
Sidewalk

こうえん
公園
Park

むら
村
Village

ちゅうしゃじょう
駐車場
Parking lot

ベンチ
Bench

がいとう
街灯
Street light

さか
坂
Slope

いなか
田舎
Countryside

けん
県
Prefecture

し
市
City

く
区
District / Ward

くに
国
Country

いりぐち
入口
Entrance

でぐち
出口
Exit

みなと
港
Port

ふんすい
噴水
Fountain

かだん
花壇
Flower bed

む
向かう
Heading

とちゅう
途中
On the way

いち
位置
Position

<ruby>東<rt>ひがし</rt></ruby>

East

<ruby>西<rt>にし</rt></ruby>

West

<ruby>南<rt>みなみ</rt></ruby>

South

<ruby>北<rt>きた</rt></ruby>

North

<ruby>右<rt>みぎ</rt></ruby>

Right

<ruby>左<rt>ひだり</rt></ruby>

Left

まっすぐ

Straight

<ruby>曲<rt>ま</rt></ruby>がる

Turn

<ruby>一方通行<rt>いっぽうつうこう</rt></ruby>

One way

<ruby>止<rt>と</rt></ruby>まれ

Stop

<ruby>方向<rt>ほうこう</rt></ruby>

Direction

<ruby>場所<rt>ばしょ</rt></ruby>

Location

<ruby>地図<rt>ちず</rt></ruby>

Map

<ruby>行<rt>い</rt></ruby>き<ruby>止<rt>ど</rt></ruby>まり

Dead end

<ruby>徐行<rt>じょこう</rt></ruby>

Slow down

<ruby>危険<rt>きけん</rt></ruby>

Dangerous

48

ちか
近い

Near

とお
遠い

Far

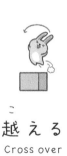

こ
越える

Cross over

あいだ
間

Between

うえ
上

Up / Above / On

した
下

Below / Under / Down

まえ
前

Front

うし
後ろ

Back / Behind

なか
中

Inside / Middle

まわ
周り

Around

うち がわ
内側

Inside

そと がわ
外側

Outside

よこ
横

Side

ここ

Here

そこ

There

あそこ

Over there

Train

えき
駅
Station

ち か てつ
地下鉄
Subway

でん しゃ
電車
Train

しん かん せん
新幹線
Bullet train

けん ばい き
券売機
Ticket vending machine

きっ ぷ
切符
Train ticket

じょう しゃ けん
乗車券
Ticket

あん ない じょ
案内所
Information center

かい さつ ぐち
改札口
Ticket gate

で ぐち
出口
Exit

ホーム
Platform

じょう きゃく
乗客
Passengers

し てい せき
指定席
Reserved seat

じ ゆう せき
自由席
Non-reserved seat

つ かわ
吊り革
Strap

アイシー
ICカード
IC card

かた みち
片道
One-way

おう ふく
往復
Round trip

じ こくひょう
時刻表
Timetable

まど ぐち
窓口
Ticket counter

くう せき
空席
Available seat

まん せき
満席
Full seat

しゃ りょう
車両
Train car

の　　か
乗り換え
Transfer trains

ふ つう れっしゃ
普通列車
Local train

かい そく れっしゃ
快速列車
Rapid train

とっきゅう れっしゃ
特急列車
Express train

てい しゃ えき
停車駅
Stop
(on a train's route)

の
乗る
Get on

お
降りる
Get off

えき べん
駅弁
Train station
boxed lunch

ろ せん ず
路線図
Route map

えきいん
駅員
Station attendant

せんろ
線路
Railway tracks

ざせき
座席
Seat

ゆうせんせき
優先席
Priority seat

しゅっぱつ
出発
Departure

とうちゃく
到着
Arrival

うんちん
運賃
Fare

ドア
Door

しはつ
始発
First train

しゅうでん
終電
Last train

い
～行き
Bound for

ていきけん
定期券
Commuter pass

て
手すり
Handrail

しゃしょう
車掌
Conductor

コインロッカー
Locker

モノレール
Monorail

Car

ハンドル
Steering wheel

タイヤ
Tire

シートベルト
Seat belt

ブレーキ
Brake

ナンバープレート
License plate

エンジン
Engine

トランク
Trunk

ワイパー
Wipers

ガソリンスタンド
Gas station

レギュラー
Unleaded

ハイオク
Premium unleaded

けい ゆ
軽油
Diesel fuel

きゅうゆ
給油
Refuel

ガソリン
Gasoline

せん しゃ
洗車
Car wash

くう き あつ
空気圧
Air pressure

Transport / Vehicles

くるま
車
Car

けい
軽トラック
Mini truck

じ てん しゃ
自転車
Bicycle

げん つき
原付
Moped

バイク
Motorcycle

トラック
Truck

パトカー
Police car

きゅう きゅう しゃ
救急車
Ambulance

ヘリコプター
Helicopter

スケボー
Skateboard

ふね
船
Ship

ヨット
Yacht

ロケット
Rocket

き しゃ
汽車
Steam train

ケーブルカー
Cable car

か もつ せん
貨物船
Cargo ship

の　もの
乗り物
Vehicles

でん しゃ
電車
Train

しん かん せん
新幹線
Bullet train

ち か てつ
地下鉄
Subway

モノレール
Monorail

バス
Bus

タクシー
Taxi

しょうぼうしゃ
消防車
Fire truck

しゅうしゅうしゃ
ゴミ収集車
Garbage truck

き きゅう
気球
Balloon

さんりん しゃ
三輪車
Tricycle

せんすいかん
潜水艦
Submarine

ベビーカー
Baby stroller

ひ こう き
飛行機
Airplane

いちりんしゃ
一輪車
Unicycle

ゆうびんしゃ
郵便車
Mail truck

Airport

ひ こう き
飛行機
Airplane

くう こう
空港
Airport

きゃく しつ じょう む いん
客室乗務員
Flight attendant

こう くう がい しゃ
航空会社
Airline company

チェックイン
Check-in

スーツケース
Suitcase

パスポート
Passport

て に もつ
手荷物
Hand luggage

ぜい かん
税関
Custom

めん ぜい てん
免税店
Duty free shop

りょう がえ じょ
両替所
Money exchange

にゅう こく しん さ
入国審査
Immigration

とう じょう じ こく
搭乗時刻
Boarding time

とう ちゃく じ こく
到着時刻
Arrival time

けっ こう
欠航
Flight cancellation

とう じょう けん
搭乗券
Boarding pass

まど がわ
窓 側
Window side

つう ろ がわ
通 路 側
Aisle side

こくない せん
国 内 線
Domestic flight

こくさい せん
国 際 線
International flight

とうじょうぐち
搭 乗 口
Boarding gate

びん めい
便 名
Flight number

き ない しょく
機 内 食
In flight meal

ひこう じ かん
飛 行 時 間
Flight time

りょけん ばん ごう
旅 券 番 号
Passport number

さん そ
酸 素 マスク
Oxygen mask

ビザ
Visa

に もつう   と
荷 物 受 け 取 り
Baggage claim

ち えん
遅 延
Delay

ターミナル
Terminal

り りく
離 陸
Takeoff

ちゃくりく
着 陸
Landing

57

Drinks

<ruby>飲<rt>の</rt></ruby> み <ruby>物<rt>もの</rt></ruby>
Drink

<ruby>水<rt>みず</rt></ruby>
Water

<ruby>炭<rt>たん</rt></ruby> <ruby>酸<rt>さん</rt></ruby> <ruby>水<rt>すい</rt></ruby>
Bubble water

<ruby>牛<rt>ぎゅう</rt></ruby> <ruby>乳<rt>にゅう</rt></ruby>
Milk

<ruby>豆<rt>とう</rt></ruby> <ruby>乳<rt>にゅう</rt></ruby>
Soy milk

サイダー
Cider

ジュース
Juice

クリームソーダ
Cream soda

ラムネ
Ramune soda

レモネード
Lemonade

コーラ
Cola

ジンジャーエール
Ginger Ale

オレンジジュース
Orange juice

スムージー
Smoothie

タピオカティー
Tapioca tea

ヤクルト
Yakult

ココア

Cocoa

コーヒー

Coffee

エスプレッソ

Espresso

カフェオレ

Cafe au lait

アイスコーヒー

Iced coffee

カップチーノ

Cappuccino

コーヒー牛乳
（ぎゅうにゅう）

Coffee milk

紅茶
（こうちゃ）

Black tea

レモンティー

Lemon tea

ミルクティー

Milk tea

アイスティー

Iced tea

抹茶
（まっちゃ）

Matcha

抹茶ラテ
（まっちゃ）

Matcha latte

緑茶
（りょくちゃ）

Green tea

烏龍茶
（うーろんちゃ）

Oolong tea

麦茶
（むぎちゃ）

Barley tea

さけ
お酒
Alcohol

に ほんしゅ
日本酒
Sake

れい しゅ
冷酒
Cold sake

あっ かん
熱燗
Hot sake

なま
生ビール
Draft beer

びん
瓶ビール
Bottled beer

ワイン
Wine

あか
赤ワイン
Red wine

しろ
白ワイン
White wine

シャンパン
Champagne

ちゅう
酎ハイ
Fruits cocktail

しょう ちゅう
焼酎
Shochu

カクテル
Cocktail

うめ しゅ
梅酒
Plum wine

ウイスキー
Whiskey

ハイボール
Whiskey and soda

60

Shopping

かね
お金
Money

げん きん
現金
Cash

クレジットカード
Credit card

ポイントカード
Point card

レシート
Receipt

つ
お釣り
Change

レジ
Cash register

ぶくろ
レジ袋
Plastic bag

ね だん
値段
Price

てん いん
店員
Clerk

う   ば
売り場
Section

しちゃくしつ
試着室
Fitting room

かみ ぶくろ
紙袋
Paper bag

きゃく
客
Customer

かご
Shopping basket

セール
Sale

わりびき
割引
Discount

カート
Shopping cart

かい てん
開店
Open

へい てん
閉店
Close

Fruits and Vegetables

くだ もの
果物
Fruits

りん ご
林檎
Apple

ぶ どう
葡萄
Grape

み かん
蜜柑
Mandarin orange

もも
桃
Peach

あお りん ご
青林檎
Green apple

ライチ
Lychee

バナナ
Banana

パッションフルーツ
Passion fruit

ココナッツ
Coconut

なし
梨
Japanese pear

レモン
Lemon

ブルーベリー
Blueberry

ブラックベリー
Blackberry

かき
柿
Persimmon

ゆ ず
柚子
Yuzu

ライム
Lime

いちじく
Fig

パパイヤ
Papaya

さくらんぼ
Cherry

ザクロ
Pomegranate

マンゴー
Mango

グレープフルーツ
Grapefruit

すもも
Plum

うめ
梅
Ume plum

オレンジ
Orange

プルーン
Prune

びわ
Loquat

キウイ
Kiwi

ようなし
洋梨
Pear

マスカット
Muscat

パイナップル
Pineapple

<ruby>蓮<rt>れん</rt></ruby><ruby>根<rt>こん</rt></ruby>
Lotus root

<ruby>茄<rt>な</rt></ruby><ruby>子<rt>す</rt></ruby>
Eggplant

かぼちゃ
Pumpkin

ピーマン
Green pepper

パプリカ
Paprika

ズッキーニ
Zucchini

とうもろこし
Corn

セロリ
Celery

<ruby>生姜<rt>しょうが</rt></ruby>
Ginger

<ruby>玉<rt>たま</rt></ruby>ねぎ
Onion

ブロッコリー
Broccoli

<ruby>枝豆<rt>えだまめ</rt></ruby>
Edamame

ニンニク
Garlic

<ruby>白菜<rt>はくさい</rt></ruby>
Chinese cabbage

もやし
Bean sprouts

ほうれん<ruby>草<rt>そう</rt></ruby>
Spinach

アボカド
Avocado

いちご
苺
Strawberry

メロン
Melon

スイカ
Watermelon

たね
種
Seed

かわ
皮
Skin

へた
Stem

かじゅう
果汁
Juice

やさい
野菜
Vegetables

トマト
Tomato

きゅうり
Cucumber

にんじん
人参
Carrot

じゃがいも
Potatoes

あお
青ネギ
Green onion

なが
長ネギ
Japanese leek

ミニトマト
Cherry tomato

さつまいも

Sweet potato

だいこん
大根

Daikon radish

レタス

Lettuce

キャベツ

Cabbage

ちんげんさい
青梗菜

Bok choy

カリフラワー

Cauliflower

さといも
里芋

Taro

にら

Garlic chives

オクラ

Okra

ながいも
長芋

Chinese yam

ごぼう

Burdock

たけのこ
筍

Bamboo shoot

まめ
インゲン豆

Green beans

シソ

Shiso

アスパラガス

Asparagus

カブ

Turnip

66

ゴーヤ

Bitter melon

しゅん ぎく
春菊

Crown daisy

とう がら し
唐辛子

Chilli pepper

ししとう

Shishito pepper

らっきょう

Japanese shallot

みょうが

Myoga ginger

み ば
三つ葉

Japanese parsley

きのこ

Mushrooms

まつ たけ
松茸

Matsutake mushroom

きくらげ

Cloud ear mushroom

えのきたけ

Enoki mushrooms

しめじ

Shimeji mushrooms

なめこ

Nameko mushrooms

しい たけ
椎茸

Shiitake mushroom

マッシュルーム

Mushroom

エリンギ

Eryngi mushrooms

Dessert

ワッフル
Waffle

わ が し
和菓子
Japanese sweets

ロールケーキ
Swiss roll

や
たい焼き
Taiyaki
(fish shaped cake
with sweet red bean
inside)

パンケーキ
Pancake

ドーナツ
Doughnut

シュークリーム
Cream puff

わた が し
綿菓子
Cotton candy

プリン
Pudding

ソフトクリーム
Soft serve ice cream

アイスクリーム
Ice cream

や
どら焼き
Dorayaki
(Red bean pancake)

だん ご
団子
Dango

エクレア
Eclair

ケーキ
Cake

カステラ
Castella

パフェ
Parfait

あんみつ
Anmitsu
(Agar cubes with sweet
red bean paste, fruits,
and syrup)

おしるこ
Oshiruko
(sweet red bean soup
with mochi)

わらび餅
もち
Warabi mochi
(mochi topped with
toasted soybean
flour)

クレープ
Crepe

マカロン
Macaron

ティラミス
Tiramisu

羊羹
ようかん
Yokan
(Azuki bean jelly)

マドレーヌ
Madeleine

アップルパイ
Apple pie

バームクーヘン
Baumkuchen

苺大福
いちご だい ふく
Strawberry red bean
rice cake

スコーン
Scone

金平糖
こん ぺい とう
Kompeito
(Japanese sugar
candy)

おはぎ
Ohagi
(Bean cake)

チーズケーキ
cheese cake

69

Meals

ラーメン
Ramen

さし み
刺 身
Sashimi

おにぎり
Rice ball

そ ば
蕎 麦
Soba
(Buckwheat noodles)

チャーハン
炒 飯
Fried rice

ぎゅうどん
牛 丼
Beef bowl

ぎょうざ
餃 子
Dumpling

カレー
Curry and rice

とんかつ
Pork cutlet

み そ しる
味 噌 汁
Miso soup

こ や
お 好 み 焼 き
Okonomiyaki
(Japanese savoury
pancake)

や
す き 焼 き
Sukiyaki
(Japanese beef hot
pot)

おでん
Oden
(Japanese stew)

から あ
唐 揚 げ
Japanese fried
chicken

や
た こ 焼 き
Takoyaki
(octopus dumpling)

おや こ どん
親 子 丼
Oyako-don
(chicken and egg
bowl)

串カツ
くし

Kushikatsu
(deep-fried skewers)

肉まん
にく

Steamed bun with
minced meat filling

ハンバーガー

Hamburger

グラタン

Gratin

オムライス

Omelette with rice

ピザ

Pizza

ポテト

French fries

サラダ

Salad

サンドイッチ

Sandwich

ステーキ

Steak

ホットドッグ

Hot dog

パスタ

Pasta

生姜焼き
しょうが や

Pork fried in ginger
sauce

肉じゃが
にく

Meat and potatoes
stew

天丼
てん どん

Tempura served over
a bowl of rice

海鮮丼
かい せん どん

Bowl of rice topped
with seafood

わしょく
和食

Japanese food

ようしょく
洋食

Western styled food

べんとう
弁当

Box lunch

そうめん
素麺

Somen noodles

や
焼きそば

Stir fried noodles
with vegetables and
meat

エビフライ

Fried shrimp

うどん

Udon noodles

や　とり
焼き鳥

Chicken skewers

うな じゅう
鰻重

Broiled eel served
over rice in a
lacquered box

しゃぶしゃぶ

Shabu-shabu
(Japanese hotpot dish
of thinly sliced meat
and vegetables)

やきにく
焼肉

Japanese BBQ

めん
つけ麺

Dipping noodles

てん
天ぷら

Tempura

ポテトサラダ

Potato salad

たまご や
卵焼き

Japanese rolled
omelette

なべ
鍋

Hot pot

Restaurant

レストラン
Restaurant

メニュー
Menu

ちゅう もん
注文 する
Order

かん ぱい
乾杯
Cheers

おすすめ
Recommendation

おしぼり
Wet towel

よ やく
予約 をする
Make a reservation

かい けい
会計 をする
Pay the bill

あじ
味
Taste

あま
甘い
Sweet

から
辛い
Spicy

す
酸っぱい
Sour

しょ
塩っぱい
Salty

にが
苦い
Bitter

お い
美味しい
Taste good

まず
不味い
It doesn't taste good

Sushi

すし
寿司
Sushi

にぎ　ずし
握り寿司
Nigirizushi

ま　ずし
巻き寿司
Rolled sushi

て ま　ずし
手巻き寿司
Hand rolled sushi

ずし
いなり寿司
Inari-zushi
(sushi wrapped in
fried tofu)

ずし
ちらし寿司
Scattered sushi

お　ずし
押し寿司
Pressed sushi

まぐろ
鮪
Tuna

サーモン
Salmon

イカ
Squid

たまご
Seasoned omelet

えび
海老
Shrimp

あじ
鯵
Horse mackerel

イクラ
Salmon roe

ウニ
Sea urchin

うなぎ
鰻
Eel

あまえび
甘海老
Sweet shrimp

タコ
Octopus

たい
鯛
Sea bream

はまち
Young yellowtail

ちゅう
中トロ
Medium fatty tuna

おお
大トロ
Fatty tuna

いわし
Sardine

かず　こ
数の子
Herring roe

えんがわ
Fluke fin

ハマグリ
Orient clam

め
芽ねぎ
Green onion

ふとま
太巻き
Thick sushi roll

てっかま
鉄火巻き
Tuna roll

ま
かっぱ巻き
Cucumber roll

ま
かんぴょう巻き
Dried gourd roll

しんこ　ま
新香巻き
Pickled radish roll

あなご
穴子
Conger eel

さんま
秋刀魚
Saury

さば
シメ鯖
Soused mackerel

ほたて
帆立
Scallop

ネギトロ
Minced fatty tuna roll

かつお
鰹
Bonito

かに
蟹
Crab

あぶ
炙りサーモン
Seared salmon

ネタ
Topping

わさび
Wasabi

ぬ
わさび抜き
Without wasabi

かん
貫
Counter for sushi

のり
海苔
Dried seaweed

しょうゆ
醤油
Soy sauce

シャリ
Vinegared rice

ガリ
Pickled ginger

Yakitori

焼き鳥

Chicken skewers

むね

Breast

ささみ

Tenderloin

砂肝

Gizzard

せせり

Neck

レバー

Liver

なんこつ

Cartilage

もも

Thigh

手羽元

Drumette

手羽中

Wingette

手羽先

Wing tip

ぼんじり

Tail

ねぎま

Thigh meat skewered
with pieces of leek

つくね

Meatball

皮

Skin

ハツ

Heart

Groceries

しょくりょうひん
食料品
Groceries

たまご
卵
Egg

チーズ
Cheese

パン
Bread

ハム
Ham

ヨーグルト
Yogurt

かん
ツナ缶
Canned tuna

しょくひん
インスタント食品
Instant food

ソーセージ
Sausage

こめ
米
Rice

にく
肉
Meat

ぎゅうにく
牛肉
Beef

とりにく
鶏肉
Chicken

ぶたにく
豚肉
Pork

ぎょかいるい
魚介類
Seafood

ぎょにく
魚肉ソーセージ
Fish sausage

まめ
豆
Beans / Pulse

なっとう
納豆
Natto

かし
お菓子
Snack

つけもの
漬物
Pickles

れいとうしょくひん
冷凍食品
Frozen foods

にゅうせいひん
乳製品
Dairy products

かこうしょくひん
加工食品
Processed foods

せいせんしょくひん
生鮮食品
Fresh foods

ナッツ
Nuts

くり
栗
Chestnut

ピーナッツ
Peanuts

クルミ
Walnut

アーモンド
Almond

ヘーゼルナッツ
Hazelnut

カシューナッツ
Cashew nut

ピスタチオ
Pistachio

ゆば
Yuba

とうふ
豆腐
Tofu

こんにゃく
Konjac

そうざい
惣菜
Side dish

こむぎこ
小麦粉
Wheat flour

かたくりこ
片栗粉
Starch

はくりきこ
薄力粉
Weak flour

きょうりきこ
強力粉
Strong flour

シリアル
Cereal

パスタ
Pasta

そば
蕎麦
Soba noodles

うどん
Udon noodles

もち
餅
Mochi

かんづめ
缶詰
Canned food

かんめん
乾麺
Dried noodles

アイス
Ice cream

ちょうみりょう
調味料
Seasoning

しお
塩
Salt

こしょう
胡椒
Pepper

さとう
砂糖
Sugar

あぶら
油
Oil

す
酢
Vinegar

わさび
Wasabi

マヨネーズ
Mayonnaise

ケチャップ
Ketchup

しょうゆ
醤油
Soy sauce

からし
辛子
Japanese mustard

みりん
Mirin (sweetened sake)

だし
Dashi (Japanese soup stock)

ごま あぶら
胡麻油
Sesame oil

オリーブオイル
Olive oil

ゆ
ラー油
Red chili oil

りょう り しゅ
料理酒
Cooking sake

ソース
Sauce

ドレッシング
Salad dressing

こう しん りょう
香辛料
Spices

み そ
味噌
Miso

バター
Butter

ジャム
Jam

は ち みつ
蜂蜜
Honey

こん ぶ
昆布
Kombu seaweed

わかめ
Wakame seaweed

かい そう
海藻
Seaweed

うめ ぼ
梅干し
Pickled plums

やき にく
焼肉のたれ
Yakiniku sauce

ふりかけ
Rice seasoning

キムチ
Kimchi

ハーブ
Herbs

Onigiri

お握り
<ruby>握<rt>にぎ</rt></ruby>

Rice ball

鮭
<ruby>鮭<rt>さけ</rt></ruby>

Salmon

梅
<ruby>梅<rt>うめ</rt></ruby>

Pickled plum

ツナマヨ

Flaked tuna mixed with mayo

おかか

Bonito flakes

炊き込みご飯
<ruby>炊<rt>た</rt></ruby><ruby>込<rt>こ</rt></ruby><ruby>飯<rt>はん</rt></ruby>

Seasoned rice with vegetables

明太子
<ruby>明<rt>めん</rt></ruby><ruby>太<rt>たい</rt></ruby><ruby>子<rt>こ</rt></ruby>

Spicy cod roe

赤飯
<ruby>赤飯<rt>せきはん</rt></ruby>

Rice with red beans

焼きおにぎり
<ruby>焼<rt>や</rt></ruby>

Grilled rice ball

塩
<ruby>塩<rt>しお</rt></ruby>

Salt (no filling)

オムライス

Omelette with rice

いくら

Salmon roe

天むす
<ruby>天<rt>てん</rt></ruby>

Deep fried shrimp

炒飯
<ruby>炒飯<rt>チャーハン</rt></ruby>

Fried rice

高菜
<ruby>高<rt>たか</rt></ruby><ruby>菜<rt>な</rt></ruby>

Leaf mustard

たらこ

Cod roe

Kitchen and Cooking

だいどころ
台所
Kitchen

れいぞうこ
冷蔵庫
Refrigerator

れいとうこ
冷凍庫
Freezer

でんし
電子レンジ
Microwave oven

オーブントースター
Toaster oven

ガスコンロ
Gas stove

すいはんき
炊飯器
Rice cooker

かんきせん
換気扇
Exhaust fan

ながだい
流し台
Sink

オーブン
Oven

しょっきあらき
食器洗い機
Dishwasher

ミキサー
Mixer

フライパン
Frying pan

なべ
鍋
Pot

ほうちょう
包丁
Knife

ざる
Colander

マグカップ

Mug

グラス

Glass

ワイングラス

Wine glass

ジョッキ

Beer mug

ゆ の
湯呑み

Handleless teacup

ティーカップ

Tea cup

りょう り
料理する

To cook

あわ だ
泡立てる

To whisk

ゆ
茹でる

To boil

き
切る

To cut

いた
炒める

To stir fry

に こ
煮込む

To stew

ま
混ぜる

To mix

や
焼く

To grill

あ
揚げる

To fry

む
蒸す

To steam

しゃもじ
Rice spoon

あわ だ き
泡立て器
Whisk

へら
Spatula

かわ む き
皮剥き器
Peeler

たま
お玉
Ladle

がえ
フライ返し
Spatula

やかん
Kettle

かん き
缶切り
Can opener

サランラップ
Plastic wrap

アルミホイル
Aluminum foil

キッチンペーパー
Kitchen paper

エプロン
Apron

けい りょう
軽量スプーン
Measuring spoon

ふ きん
布巾
Dish towel

しょっき せん ざい
食器洗剤
Dish soap

べん とう ばこ
弁当箱
Lunch box

86

はかり
Kitchen scale

ケトル
Electric kettle

ハンドブレンダー
Immersion blender

まな板
Cutting board

ワインオープナー
Wine opener

栓抜き
Bottle opener

急須
Teapot

鍋つかみ
Oven mitt

箸
Chopsticks

スプーン
Spoon

フォーク
Fork

ナイフ
Knife

皿
Dish

茶碗
Rice bowl

食器
Tableware

ラーメン鉢
Ramen bowl

House

いえ
家
House

げん かん
玄関
Front door

や ね
屋根
Roof

えん とつ
煙突
Chimney

まど
窓
Window

ドア
Door

てんじょう
天井
Ceiling

か べ
壁
Wall

しゃ こ
車庫
Garage

にわ
庭
Garden

いぬ ご や
犬小屋
Kennel

へ や
部屋
Room

ゆか
床
Floor

バルコニー
Balcony

だん ろ
暖炉
Fireplace

だんぼう
暖房
Heater

たな
棚
Shelf

ソファー
Couch

かぎ
鍵
Key

ひ　だ
引き出し
Drawer

でん わ
電話
Telephone

と けい
時計
Clock

ぬいぐるみ
Stuffed animal

カーテン
Curtain

ほん だな
本棚
Bookshelf

ドレッサー
Dresser

ラグ
Rug

つくえ
机
Desk

ベッド
Bed

テーブル
Table

い す
椅子
Chair

れい ぼう
冷房
Air conditioner

テレビ
TV

リモコン
Remote control

コンセント
Outlets

でんき
電気
Electricity

スピーカー
Speaker

ヒーター
Heater

かしつき
加湿器
Humidifier

ストーブ
Stove

おくじょう
屋上
Rooftop

かがみ
鏡
Mirror

かいだん
階段
Stairs

かぐ
家具
Furniture

でんき
電気スイッチ
Light switch

でんきゅう
電球
Light bulb

でんち
電池
Battery

けいたいでんわ
携帯電話
スマホ
Cell phone
Smartphone

わしつ
和室
Japanese style room

おしいれ
押入れ
Closet

たたみ
畳
Tatami

ふすま
Fusuma (sliding doors)

ふとん
布団
Futon

か　ぶとん
掛け布団
Comforter

まくら
枕
Pillow

しょうじ
障子
Shoji (paper sliding doors)

こたつ
Kotatsu

か　じく
掛け軸
Hanging scroll

ざ　ぶとん
座布団
Sitting cushion

せんぷうき
扇風機
Electric fan

か びん
花瓶
Vase

しょくぶつ
植物
Plant

こう
お香
Incense

しょうめい
照明
Lighting

Cleaning

そうじ ようぐ
掃除用具
Cleaning tools

そうじき
掃除機
Vacuum

ほうき
Broom

ちりとり
Dust pan

ぞうきん
雑巾
Cleaning cloth

てぶくろ
ゴム手袋
Rubber gloves

バケツ
Bucket

モップ
Mop

たわし
Scrubber

スポンジ
Sponge

はたき
Duster

じゅうそう
重曹
Baking soda

アイロン
Iron

だい
アイロン台
Iron board

し
染み
Stain

し ぬ
染み抜き
Stain remover

せんたくき
洗濯機
Washing machine

せんたくもの
洗濯物
Laundry

せんたく
洗濯かご
Laundry basket

せんたくせんざい
洗濯洗剤
Laundry detergent

ひょうはくざい
漂白剤
Bleach

じゅうなんざい
柔軟剤
Softener

せんたくひょうじ
洗濯表示
Laundry labels

せんたく
洗濯ばさみ
Clothes peg

ほこり
埃
Dust

カビ
Mold

じょきん
除菌スプレー
Sanitize Spray

ぼう
防カビスプレー
Anti mold spray

ばこ
ゴミ箱
Garbage can

ぶくろ
ゴミ袋
Garbage bag

も
燃えるゴミ
Burnable garbage

も
燃えないゴミ
Non-burnable
garbage

なま
生ゴミ

Compost

しげん
資源ゴミ

Recyclable trash

そだい
粗大ゴミ

Bulky trash

こし
古紙

Papers for recycling

そうじ
掃除する

To clean

そうじき
掃除機をかける

To vacuum

は
掃く

To sweep

アイロンをかける

Ironing clothes

ふく
服をたたむ

To fold clothes

ふ
拭く

To wipe

こする

To rub

せいり
整理する

To tidy up

せんたくもの ほ
洗濯物を干す

To hang the laundry

かんき
換気する

To ventilate

かがみ みが
鏡を磨く

To polish a mirror

くつ みが
靴を磨く

To polish one's shoes

Toilet

トイレ / 手洗い
Toilet

トイレットペーパー
Toilet paper

便器
Toilet bowl

便座
Toilet seat

うんち / うんこ
Poop

おしっこ
Pee

流す
to Flush

大
Flush

小
Light flush

止
To stop

おしり
Rear

やわらか
Light Rear

ビデ
Front

音
Sound (Privacy)

乾燥
Dry

温度設定
Temperature setting

Bath

お風呂
<ruby>ふ<rt></rt></ruby> <ruby>ろ<rt></rt></ruby>
Bath

浴槽
よく そう
Bathtub

シャワー
Shower

水
みず
Water

お湯
ゆ
Hot water

シャンプー
Shampoo

リンス
Conditioner

ボディーソープ
Body soap

石鹸
せっ けん
Soap

洗面器
せん めん き
Washbowl

洗面台
せん めん だい
Bathroom sink

体重計
たい じゅう けい
Weight scales

バスタオル
Bath towel

鏡
かが み
Mirror

爪切り
つめ き
Nail clippers

入浴剤
にゅう よく ざい
Bath bomb

バスマット
Bath mat

あわ
泡
Bubbles

クシ
Comb

めんぼう
綿棒
Cotton swab

じゃぐち
蛇口
Faucet

でんき
電気シェーバー
Electric shaver

ひげ　そ
髭を剃る
To shave

かみそり
Razor

にゅうよく
入浴
Take a bath

ドライヤー
Hair dryer

は
歯ブラシ
Toothbrush

は みが　こ
歯磨き粉
Toothpaste

ふろ　はい
お風呂に入る
Take a bath

あ
シャワーを浴びる
Take a shower

からだ あら
体を洗う
To wash one's body

は　みが
歯を磨く
To brush one's teeth

Beauty

_{け しょう すい}
化粧水
Lotion

_{にゅう えき}
乳液
Milky lotion

_{ほ しつ ざい}
保湿剤
Moisture lotion

_{び よう えき}
美容液
Serum

パック
Face mask

_{ひ や ど}
日焼け止め
Sunscreen

_{け しょう した じ}
化粧下地
Primer

_{くち べに}
口紅
Lipstick

マニキュア
Nailpolish

_{け しょう お}
化粧落とし
Makeup remover

_{せん がん}
洗顔
Face wash

_{がみ}
あぶらとり紙
Oil blotting sheets

_{け しょう}
化粧
Makeup

デオドラント
Deodorant

アイシャドウ
Eye shadow

マスカラ
Mascara

ビューラー
Eyelash curler

こうすい
香水
Perfume

びんかんはだ
敏感肌
Sensitive skin

かんそうはだ
乾燥肌
Dry skin

チーク
Blush

リップスティック
Lip balm

コンシーラー
Concealer

パウダー
Powder

ファンデーション
Foundation

アイブロウ
Eye brow

アイライナー
Eyeliner

つ
付けまつげ
False eyelashes

けしょうひん
化粧品
Cosmetics

リップグロス
Lip gloss

じょこうえき
除光液
Remover

けしょう
化粧ブラシ
Cosmetic brush

Nature and Weather

しぜん
自然
Nature

やま
山
Mountain

かわ
川
River

たに
谷
Valley

うみ
海
Ocean

みずうみ
湖
Lake

ぬま
沼
Swamp

おか
丘
Hill

たき
滝
Waterfall

どうくつ
洞窟
Cave

おんせん
温泉
Hot spring

しま
島
Island

さばく
砂漠
Desert

かいがん
海岸
Seashore

いし
石
Stone

すな
砂
Sand

き
木
Tree

はやし
林
Woods

もり
森
Forest

とち
土地
Land

みず
水
Water

たけ
竹
Bamboo

は
葉
Leaf

はな
花
Flower

つち
土
Soil

なみ
波
Wave

いけ
池
Pond

かざん
火山
Volcano

くさ
草
Grass

いわ
岩
Rock

た　た
田 / 田んぼ
Rice field

はたけ
畑
Field

がけ
崖
Cliff

かい すい
海水
Sea water

えだ
枝
Branch

さくら
桜
Cherry blossom

さん みゃく
山脈
Mountain range

そうげん
草原
Meadow

ひょうが
氷河
Glacier

お がわ
小川
Stream

にじ
虹
Rainbow

くも
雲
Cloud

かぜ
風
Wind

そら
空
Sky

くう き
空気
Air

あさ ひ
朝日
Sunrise

ゆう ひ
夕日
Sunset

オーロラ
Aurora

てん き
天気
Weather

てん き よ ほう
天気予報
Weather Forecast

き おん
気温
Temperature

しっ ど
湿度
Humidity

は
晴れ
Sunny

くも
曇り
Cloudy

あめ
雨
Rain

ゆき
雪
Snow

かみなり
雷
Thunder

あらし
嵐
Storm

きり
霧
Fog

こう すい りょう
降水量
Rainfall

あつ
暑い
Hot

さむ
寒い
Cold

む あつ
蒸し暑い
Hot and humid

すず
涼しい
Cool

Natural resources

てん ねん し げん
天 然 資 源
Natural Resources

せき ゆ
石 油
Petroleum

せき たん
石 炭
Coal

たい き
大 気
Atmosphere

きん
金
Gold

ぎん
銀
Silver

どう
銅
Copper

てつ
鉄
Iron

たい よう こう
太 陽 光
Sunlight

ウラン
Uranium

ダイアモンド
Diamond

ニッケル
Nickel

ふう りょく はつ でん
風 力 発 電
Wind power

すい りょく はつ でん
水 力 発 電
Hydroelectric power

ち ねつ はつ でん
地 熱 発 電
Geothermal power

はつ でん
バイオマス発 電
Biomass energy

Natural disasters

さい がい
災害
Disaster

じ しん
地震
Earthquake

たい ふう
台風
Typhoon

つ な み
津波
Tsunami

おお あめ
大雨
Heavy rain

こう ずい
洪水
Flood

な だ
雪崩れ
Avalanche

ふん か
噴火
Volcanic eruption

ど しゃ くず
土砂崩れ
Landslide

か じ
火事
Fire

てい でん
停電
Power outage

ひ なん
避難
Evacuation

ひ がい
被害
Damage

たつ まき
竜巻
Tornado

しん すい
浸水
Be flooded

じ すべ
地滑り
Landslide

Space

うちゅう
宇宙
Universe

たいよう
太陽
The sun

つき
月
Moon

ほし
星
Star

わくせい
惑星
Planet

ちきゅう
地球
Earth

かせい
火星
Mars

すいせい
水星
Mercury

もくせい
木星
Jupiter

きんせい
金星
Venus

どせい
土星
Saturn

てんのうせい
天王星
Uranus

かいおうせい
海王星
Neptune

みかづき
三日月
Crescent Moon

うちゅうじん
宇宙人
Alien

ながぼし
流れ星
Shooting star

ぎんがけい
銀河系
Galaxy

げっしょく
月食
Lunar eclipse

にっしょく
日食
Solar eclipse

まんげつ
満月
Full moon

Zodiac sign

せいざ
星座
Zodiac sign

おひつじざ
牡羊座
Aries

おうしざ
牡牛座
Taurus

ふたござ
双子座
Gemini

かにざ
蟹座
Cancer

ししざ
獅子座
Leo

おとめざ
乙女座
Virgo

てんびんざ
天秤座
Libra

さそりざ
蠍座
Scorpio

いてざ
射手座
Sagittarius

やぎざ
山羊座
Capricorn

みずがめざ
水瓶座
Aquarius

うおざ
魚座
Pisces

ほしうらな
星占い
Horoscope

てんたいかんそく
天体観測
Astronomical
observation

あまがわ
天の川
Milky Way

107

School

がっこう
学校
School

せんせい
先生
Teacher

せいと
生徒
Student

こうちょう
校長
Principal

ほいくえん
保育園
Nursery school

ようちえん
幼稚園
Kindergarten

しょうがっこう
小学校
Elementary school

ちゅうがっこう
中学校
Junior high school

こうこう
高校
High school

だいがく
大学
University

せんもんがっこう
専門学校
Vocational school

きょういく
教育
Education

こうもん
校門
School gate

こうてい
校庭
School yard

にゅうがく
入学
Start school

そつぎょう
卒業
Graduation

じ かん わり
時 間 割
Timetable

こくばん
黒板
Blackboard

きょう か しょ
教 科 書
Textbooks

つうちひょう
通 知 表
Report card

きょう か
教 科
Subject

やす　じ かん
休み時間
Recess time

じゅ ぎょう
授 業
Class

ほう か ご
放 課 後
After school

すう がく
数 学
Mathematics

えい ご
英 語
English

か がく
科 学
Science

れき し
歴 史
History

び じゅつ
美 術
Art

たい いく
体 育
Gym

おん がく
音 楽
Music

ず こう
図工
Arts and Crafts

きょうしつ
教室
Classroom

ほけんしつ
保健室
School infirmary

しょくいんしつ
職員室
Staff room

たいいくかん
体育館
Gymnasium

せいふく
制服
Uniforms

うわば
上履き
School indoor shoes

しゅくだい
宿題
Homework

ランドセル
School bag

きゅうしょく
給食
School lunch

テスト
Test

じしょ
辞書
Dictionary

チョーク
Chalk

なふだ
名札
Name tag

せんぱい
先輩
Senior

こうはい
後輩
Junior

がくねん
学年
Grade

ようち えんじ
幼稚園児
Kindergarten children

しょう がく せい
小学生
Elementary school students

ちゅう がく せい
中学生
Junior high school students

こうこうせい
高校生
High school students

だい がく せい
大学生
University students

よ しゅう
予習
Studying in advance

ふく しゅう
復習
To review the lesson

しゅっ せき
出席
Attendance

けっ せき
欠席
Absent

ち こく
遅刻
To be late

ごう かく
合格
Pass the test

えん そく
遠足
Excursion

しゅう がく りょ こう
修学旅行
Field trip

せい せき
成績
School grades

たい いく さい
体育祭
Sports day

ぶん か さい
文化祭
School festival

＋

<ruby>足<rt>た</rt></ruby> し <ruby>算<rt>ざん</rt></ruby>
Addition

−

<ruby>引<rt>ひ</rt></ruby> き <ruby>算<rt>ざん</rt></ruby>
Subtraction

✕

<ruby>掛<rt>か</rt></ruby> け <ruby>算<rt>ざん</rt></ruby>
Multiplication

÷

<ruby>割<rt>わ</rt></ruby> り <ruby>算<rt>ざん</rt></ruby>
Division

<ruby>偶<rt>ぐう</rt></ruby> <ruby>数<rt>すう</rt></ruby>
Even numbers

<ruby>奇<rt>き</rt></ruby> <ruby>数<rt>すう</rt></ruby>
Odd numbers

$$\frac{2}{3}$$

<ruby>分<rt>ぶん</rt></ruby> <ruby>数<rt>すう</rt></ruby>
Fraction

3.14

<ruby>小<rt>しょう</rt></ruby> <ruby>数<rt>すう</rt></ruby> <ruby>点<rt>てん</rt></ruby>
Decimal point

mm

ミリメートル
Millimeter

cm

センチメートル
Centimeter

m

メートル
Meter

km

キロメートル
Kilometer

mg

ミリグラム
Milligram

g

グラム
Gram

kg

キログラム
Kilogram

ton

トン
Ton

Shapes

かたち
形
Shape

さんかくけい
三角形
Triangle

しかくけい
四角形
Square

まる
丸
Circle

がた
ひし形
Diamond

えんけい
だ円形
Oval

ごかくけい
五角形
Pentagon

ろっかくけい
六角形
Hexagon

ちょうほうけい
長方形
Rectangle

だいけい
台形
Trapezoid

えんちゅう
円柱
Column

りっぽうたい
立方体
Cube

えん
円すい
Cone

ほしがた
星型
Star shape

がた
ハート型
Heart shape

おうぎがた
扇形
Fan shape

Computer

パソコン
Computer

キーボード
Keyboard

インターネット
Internet

マウス
Mouse

プリンター
Printer

じゅうでんき
充電器
Battery charger

でんげん
電源
Power

がめん
画面
Screen

きどう
起動する
Start up

シャットダウン
Shut down

ログイン
Log in

ログアウト
Logout

ダウンロード
Download

パスワード
Password

メール
Email

メールアドレス
Email address

Punctuation Marks

<ruby>矢<rt>や</rt>印<rt>じるし</rt></ruby>

やじるし
矢印
Arrow

せん
線
Line

なみ せん
波線
Wave dash

まる
丸
Period

かっこ
括弧
Parentheses

なみ かっこ
波括弧
Curly brackets

かぎ かっこ
鉤括弧
Japanese style
quotation marks

なか てん
中点
Bullet point

てん
点
Comma

はてなマーク
Question mark

びっくりマーク
Exclamation mark

こめじるし
米印
Japanese style
asterisk

アンダーバー
Under score

アットマーク
At sign

シャープ
Sharp / number sign

スラッシュ
Slash

Stationery

ぶんぼうぐ
文房具
Stationery

えんぴつ
鉛筆
Pencil

け
消しゴム
Eraser

ペン
Pen

シャーペン
Mechanical pencil

けいこう
蛍光ペン
Highlighter

ふでばこ
筆箱
Pencil case

てちょう
手帳
Planner

セロハンテープ
Scotch tape

はさみ
Scissors

カッター
Cutter

ノート
Notebook

かみ
紙
Paper

でんたく
電卓
Calculator

えんぴつけず
鉛筆削り
Pencil sharpener

コンパス
Compass

ファイル

File

はんこ

Stamp

<ruby>押<rt>お</rt></ruby>しピン

Tack

<ruby>封筒<rt>ふうとう</rt></ruby>

Envelope

ハガキ

Postcard

<ruby>手紙<rt>てがみ</rt></ruby>

Letter

<ruby>修正<rt>しゅうせい</rt></ruby>テープ

Correction tape

クリップ

Clip

<ruby>三角定規<rt>さんかくじょうぎ</rt></ruby>

Set square

<ruby>分度器<rt>ぶんどき</rt></ruby>

Protractor

<ruby>切手<rt>きって</rt></ruby>

Stamp

<ruby>万年筆<rt>まんねんひつ</rt></ruby>

Fountain pen

<ruby>磁石<rt>じしゃく</rt></ruby>

Magnet

シール

Sticker

<ruby>本<rt>ほん</rt></ruby>

Book

<ruby>穴<rt>あな</rt></ruby>あけパンチ

Hole puncher

ホチキス
Stapler

ホチキスの芯
Staple

付箋
Label

のり
Glue

油性ペン
Permanent marker

水性ペン
Non-permanent marker

ガムテープ
Duct tape

輪ゴム
Rubber band

定規
Ruler

色鉛筆
Colored pencils

クレヨン
Crayons

折り紙
Origami paper

しおり
Bookmark

絵の具
Paint

接着剤
Super glue

虫眼鏡
Magnifying glass

Colors

しろ
白
White

くろ
黒
Black

あお
青
Blue

あか
赤
Red

き
黄
Yellow

みどり
緑
Green

ちゃ
茶
Brown

むらさき
紫
Purple

オレンジ
Orange

ピンク
Pink

グレー
Gray

きみどり
黄緑
Light green

みず いろ
水色
Water blue

ぎん
銀
Silver

きん
金
Gold

いろ
色
Color

Occupation

きょうし
教師
Teacher

いしゃ
医者
Doctor

かんごし
看護師
Nurse

じゅうい
獣医
Veterinarian

べんごし
弁護士
Lawyer

さいばんかん
裁判官
Judge

きしゃ
記者
Reporter

せいじか
政治家
Politician

けんちくか
建築家
Architect

だいく
大工
Carpenter

けいさつかん
警察官
Police officer

しょうぼうし
消防士
Firefighter

やくしゃ
役者
Actor

モデル
Model

デザイナー
Designer

カメラマン
Photographer

<ruby>会<rt>かい</rt>社<rt>しゃ</rt>員<rt>いん</rt></ruby>

Company employee

<ruby>運<rt>うん</rt>転<rt>てん</rt>手<rt>しゅ</rt></ruby>

Driver

<ruby>会<rt>かい</rt>計<rt>けい</rt>士<rt>し</rt></ruby>

Accountant

<ruby>研<rt>けん</rt>究<rt>きゅう</rt>者<rt>しゃ</rt></ruby>

Researcher

<ruby>料<rt>りょう</rt>理<rt>り</rt>人<rt>にん</rt></ruby>

Chef

パティシエ

Patissier

<ruby>歌<rt>か</rt>手<rt>しゅ</rt></ruby>

Singer

<ruby>美<rt>び</rt>容<rt>よう</rt>師<rt>し</rt></ruby>

Hairdresser

パイロット

Pilot

<ruby>客<rt>きゃ</rt>室<rt>くしつ</rt>乗<rt>じょう</rt>務<rt>む</rt>員<rt>いん</rt></ruby>

Flight attendant

<ruby>宇<rt>う</rt>宙<rt>ちゅう</rt>飛<rt>ひ</rt>行<rt>こう</rt>士<rt>し</rt></ruby>

Astronaut

<ruby>販<rt>はん</rt>売<rt>ばい</rt>員<rt>いん</rt></ruby>

Salesperson

<ruby>声<rt>せい</rt>優<rt>ゆう</rt></ruby>

Voice actor

<ruby>漁<rt>りょう</rt>師<rt>し</rt></ruby>

Fisherman

<ruby>画<rt>が</rt>家<rt>か</rt></ruby>

Painter

<ruby>農<rt>のう</rt>家<rt>か</rt></ruby>

Farmer

Sports

スポーツ
Sports

サッカー
Soccer

野球
<ruby>や<rt></rt></ruby>きゅう
Baseball

テニス
Tennis

バレーボール
Volley ball

とざん
登山
Mountain climbing

サーフィン
Surfing

ゴルフ
Golf

たいそう
体操
Gymnastics

バドミントン
Badminton

ダイビング
Diving

ボクシング
Boxing

ランニング
Running

きん
筋トレ
Workout

ヨガ
Yoga

サイクリング
Cycling

すい えい
水 泳
Swimming

スキー
Ski

ラグビー
Rugby

バスケットボール
Basketball

たっ きゅう
卓 球
Table tennis

スノーボード
Snowboard

スケート
Skate

ウォーキング
Walking

レスリング
Wrestling

カヌー
Canoe

マラソン
Marathon

アイスホッケー
Ice hockey

りくじょう きょうぎ
陸 上 競 技
Track and field

けん どう
剣 道
Kendo

じゅう どう
柔 道
Judo

から て
空 手
Karate

ボール
Ball

バット
Bat

ラケット
Racket

スノーボード
Snowboard

グローブ
Glove

ゴルフクラブ
Golf club

ヘルメット
Helmet

ゴーグル
Goggles

ダンベル
Dumbbell

プール
Pool

<ruby>水<rt>みず</rt></ruby><ruby>着<rt>ぎ</rt></ruby>
Swimsuit

ビート<ruby>板<rt>ばん</rt></ruby>
Swimming board

シャトル
Shuttlecock

<ruby>弓<rt>ゆみ</rt></ruby>
Bow

<ruby>矢<rt>や</rt></ruby>
Arrow

<ruby>縄<rt>なわ</rt></ruby><ruby>跳<rt>と</rt></ruby>び
Jump rope

Tools

こうぐ
工具
Tools

メジャー
Measure

もっこうよう
木工用ボンド
Wood bond

ハンマー
Hammer

のこぎり
Saw

おの
斧
Axe

ペンチ
Pilers

でんき
電気ドリル
Electric drill

ドライバー
Screwdriver

ペンキ
Paint

ブラシ
Brush

やすり
File / Rasp

ナット
Nut

くぎ
釘
Nail

ネジ
Screw

すいじゅんき
水準器
Level

Hobby

しゅみ
趣味
Hobby

えいが
映画
Movie

キャンプ
Camping

どくしょ
読書
Reading

ダンス
Dancing

さいほう
裁縫
Sewing

コンサート
Concert

え か
絵を描く
Painting

か てい さい えん
家庭菜園
Home gardening

りょうり
料理
Cooking

しょどう
書道
Calligraphy

しゃしん
写真
Photography

じょうば
乗馬
Horse riding

ビデオゲーム
Video game

つ
釣り
Fishing

にちようだいく
日曜大工
DIY

おんがく
音楽
Music

ドライブ
Driving

ごがくがくしゅう
語学学習
Language learning

かもの
ショッピング/買い物
Shopping

かづく
お菓子作り
Making sweets

カラオケ
Karaoke

まんがよ
漫画を読む
Reading manga

アニメをみる
Watching anime

チェス
Playing chess

ルーレット
Roulette

トランプ
Playing cards

オセロ
Othello

ハイキング
Hiking

ファッション
Fashion

りょこう
旅行
Traveling

さんぽ
散歩
Go for a walk

ピアノ
Piano

がっき
楽器
Musical instruments

マイク
Microphone

ギター
Guitar

ヴァイオリン
Violin

フルート
Flute

リコーダー
Recorder

スピーカー
Speaker

しゃしん
写真
Photo

はり
針
Needle

いと
糸
Thread

けいと
毛糸
Yarn

ルアー
Lure

つ ざお
釣り竿
Fishing rod

ふで
筆
Writing brush

しょうせつ
小説
Novel

じょうろ
Watering can

しょくぶつ
植物
Plant

はち
鉢
Pot

スコップ
Trowel

テント
Tent

ね ぶくろ
寝袋
Sleeping bag

ロープ
Rope

かい ちゅう でん とう
懐中電灯
Flashlight

おもちゃ
Toy

ねん ど
粘土
Clay

にん ぎょう
人形
Doll

ぬいぐるみ
Stuffed animal

サイコロ
Dice

たけ うま
竹馬
Stilts

ぬ え
塗り絵
Coloring book

え ほん
絵本
Picture book

Culture

おんせん
温泉
Hot spring

きもの
着物
Kimono

さどう
茶道
Tea ceremony

いばな
生け花
Flower arrangement

ゆかた
浴衣
Yukata

ぼんさい
盆栽
Bonsai

しょうぎ
将棋
Japanese chess

こけし
Kokeshi wooden doll

しょどう
書道
Japanese calligraphy

はいく
俳句
Haiku poem

こま
Spinning top

そろばん
Abacus

しゃみせん
三味線
Three-stringed
Japanese guitar

うきよえ
浮世絵
Color print of
everyday life in the
Edo period

はなふだ
花札
Floral playing cards

だま
けん玉
Japanese bilboquet

<ruby>神<rt>じん</rt>社<rt>じゃ</rt></ruby>
Shinto shrine

<ruby>寺<rt>てら</rt></ruby>
Temple

<ruby>城<rt>しろ</rt></ruby>
Castle

すもう
Sumo

<ruby>柔<rt>じゅう</rt>道<rt>どう</rt></ruby>
Judo

<ruby>剣<rt>けん</rt>道<rt>どう</rt></ruby>
Kendo

<ruby>空<rt>から</rt>手<rt>て</rt></ruby>
Karate

<ruby>囲<rt>い</rt>碁<rt>ご</rt></ruby>
Go

<ruby>和<rt>わ</rt>紙<rt>し</rt></ruby>
Japanese paper

<ruby>落<rt>らく</rt>語<rt>ご</rt></ruby>
Traditional Japanese
comic storytelling

<ruby>漫<rt>まん</rt>才<rt>ざい</rt></ruby>
Two-person comedy
act

<ruby>琴<rt>こと</rt></ruby>
Koto

おみくじ
Fortune slip

<ruby>お守<rt>まも</rt>り</ruby>
Good luck charm

<ruby>絵<rt>え</rt>馬<rt>ま</rt></ruby>
Votive picture

<ruby>鳥<rt>とり</rt>居<rt>い</rt></ruby>
Torii gate

だるま
Daruma doll

まね　ねこ
招き猫
Beckoning cat

けん
剣
Sword

ふうりん
風鈴
Wind bell

わ　が　し
和菓子
Japanese sweets

せん　す
扇子
Folding fan

かんざし
Ornate hairpin

ふ　ろ　しき
風呂敷
Wrapping cloth

げい　しゃ
芸者
Geisha

てん　ぐ
天狗
Long-nosed goblin

まっ　ちゃ
抹茶
Matcha

こ　みん　か
古民家
Old folk house

ヨーヨー
Water balloon

ちょうちん
Paper lantern

のれん
Goodwill

しゅりけん
Shuriken

とうげい
陶芸
Ceramic art

か ぶ き
歌舞伎
Kabuki

カルタ
Traditional Japanese
playing cards

のう
能
Noh theatre

て だま
お手玉
Beanbag juggling
game

お がみ
折り紙
Origami paper folding

むかし ばなし
昔話
Folktale

だい ぶつ
大仏
Large statue of
Buddha

ぞうり
草履
Japanese traditional
sandals

うちわ
Paper fan

きゅうどう
弓道
Japanese archery

わ だい こ
和太鼓
Japanese drum

にん じゃ
忍者
Ninja

たこ
凧
Kite

ぶ し
武士
Samurai

すい ぼく が
水墨画
Ink painting

133

Verbs

い
行く
Go

く
来る
Come

ある
歩く
Walk

はし
走る
Run

あ
上がる
Go up

お
下りる
Go down

のぼ
登る
Climb

お
落ちる
Fall

か
借りる
Rent / Borrow

か
貸す
Lend

おし
教える
Teach

まな
学ぶ
Learn

お
押す
Push

ひ
引く
Pull

か
買う
Buy

う
売る
Sell

つく
作る
Make

こわ
壊す
Break

き
着る
Put on

ぬ
脱ぐ
Take off

た
立つ
Stand

すわ
座る
Sit

つける
Turn on

け
消す
Turn off

い
生きる
Live

し
死ぬ
Die

ひろ
拾う
Pick up

す
捨てる
Throw away

はじ
始める
Start

お
終える
Finish

い
入れる
Put in

だ
出す
Take out

<ruby>乗<rt>の</rt></ruby>る
Get on

<ruby>降<rt>お</rt></ruby>りる
Get off

<ruby>開<rt>あ</rt></ruby>ける
Open

<ruby>閉<rt>し</rt></ruby>める
Close

<ruby>起<rt>お</rt></ruby>きる
Get up / Wake up

<ruby>寝<rt>ね</rt></ruby>る
Go to bed / Sleep

<ruby>働<rt>はたら</rt></ruby>く
Work

<ruby>休<rt>やす</rt></ruby>む
Rest

<ruby>持<rt>も</rt></ruby>っていく
Take

<ruby>持<rt>も</rt></ruby>ってくる
Bring

<ruby>入<rt>はい</rt></ruby>る
Enter

<ruby>出<rt>で</rt></ruby>る
Go out

<ruby>忘<rt>わす</rt></ruby>れる
Forget

<ruby>覚<rt>おぼ</rt></ruby>える
Memorise / Remember

<ruby>勝<rt>か</rt></ruby>つ
Win

<ruby>負<rt>ま</rt></ruby>ける
Lose

136

いわ
祝う
Celebrate

ぬす
盗む
Steal

も
持つ
Have / Hold

はら
払う
Pay

し
知る
Know

と
止まる
Stop

ま
待つ
Wait

なら
並ぶ
Line up

ひ こ
引っ越す
Move (House)

ほ
欲しい
Want

じゅん び
準備する
Prepare

しょうかい
紹介する
Introduce

よ やく
予約する
To make a
reservation /
To book

かえる
Change

せつ めい
説明する
Explain

こた
答える
Answer

<ruby>送<rt>おく</rt></ruby>る
Send

<ruby>飛<rt>と</rt></ruby>ぶ
Fly

<ruby>泳<rt>およ</rt></ruby>ぐ
Swim

<ruby>話<rt>はな</rt></ruby>す
Talk / Speak

<ruby>食<rt>た</rt></ruby>べる
Eat

<ruby>飲<rt>の</rt></ruby>む
Drink

<ruby>会<rt>あ</rt></ruby>う
Meet

<ruby>着<rt>つ</rt></ruby>く
Arrive

<ruby>思<rt>おも</rt></ruby>う
Think

<ruby>思<rt>おも</rt></ruby>い<ruby>出<rt>だ</rt></ruby>す
Recall

<ruby>分<rt>わ</rt></ruby>かる
Understand

<ruby>見<rt>み</rt></ruby>る
See / Look / Watch

<ruby>遊<rt>あそ</rt></ruby>ぶ
Play

<ruby>頼<rt>たの</rt></ruby>む
Ask

<ruby>洗<rt>あら</rt></ruby>う
Wash

<ruby>手伝<rt>てつだ</rt></ruby>う
Help

き
聞く
Listen / Hear /Ask

い
言う
Say

うた
歌う
Sing

か
書く
Write

よ
読む
Read

えら
選ぶ
Choose / Select

お
置く
Put

かえ
返す
Return

み
見つける
Find

つか
使う
Use

べん きょう
勉強 する
Study

りょこう
旅行 する
Travel

うん てん
運転 する
Drive

よ
呼ぶ
Call

き
切る
Cut

すべ
滑る
Slide

あやま
謝る
Apologize

せ わ
世話をする
Look after
Take care of

まわ
回る
Spin

かざ
飾る
decorate

な
失くす
Lose something

まちが
間違える
Mistake

じゃま
邪魔する
Disturb

とお
通る
Go through

わ
割れる
Break /Smash /Crack

な
投げる
Throw

たた
叩く
Knock

ゆ
揺れる
Shake

う
植える
Plant

れん しゅう
練習する
Practice

う と
受け取る
Receive

おく
贈る
Give a present

<ruby>楽<rt>たの</rt></ruby>しむ

Enjoy

<ruby>住<rt>す</rt></ruby>む

Live

<ruby>愛<rt>あい</rt></ruby>する

Love

する

Do

<ruby>信<rt>しん</rt></ruby>じる

Believe

<ruby>決<rt>き</rt></ruby>める

Decide

<ruby>試<rt>ため</rt></ruby>す

Try

<ruby>数<rt>かぞ</rt></ruby>える

Count

<ruby>弾<rt>ひ</rt></ruby>く

Play (guitar, piano etc)

<ruby>貼<rt>は</rt></ruby>る

Stick / Paste

<ruby>撮<rt>と</rt></ruby>る

Take (a picture)

<ruby>干<rt>ほ</rt></ruby>す

Dry

<ruby>磨<rt>みが</rt></ruby>く

Polish

<ruby>剥<rt>む</rt></ruby>く

Peel

<ruby>競<rt>きそ</rt></ruby>う

Compete with

<ruby>失敗<rt>しっぱい</rt></ruby>する

Fail

Emotions and Feelings

うれ
嬉しい
Happy

たの
楽しい
Fun

つまらない
Boring

かな
悲しい
Sad

おも しろ
面白い
Funny / Interesting

こわい
Scary

は
恥ずかしい
Embarrassing

つら
辛い
Tough / Hard

さび
寂しい
Lonely

しん ぱい
心配
Worry

がっかり
Be disappointed

あん しん
安心
Relief

おこ
怒る
Angry

お こ
落ち込む
Feel down

わら
笑う
Laugh

うらや
羨ましい
Envious

つか
疲れた
Tired

しあわ
幸せ
Happiness

なか
お腹すいた
Hungry

のど かわ
喉乾いた
Thirsty

ねむ
眠い
Sleepy

ふ あん
不安
Anxiety

あきれる
Be astounded

きん ちょう
緊張する
Nervous

いそが
忙しい
Busy

ひま
暇
Be bored

びっくり
Be surprised

かん どう
感動
Impress

なつ
懐かしい
Nostalgic

くや
悔しい
Frustrating

あせ
焦る
Panic

こう かい
後悔
Regret

Opposites

<ruby>大<rt>おお</rt></ruby>きい

Big

<ruby>小<rt>ちい</rt></ruby>さい

Small

<ruby>多<rt>おお</rt></ruby>い

Many

<ruby>少<rt>すく</rt></ruby>ない

Few

<ruby>高<rt>たか</rt></ruby>い

Expensive

<ruby>安<rt>やす</rt></ruby>い

Cheap

<ruby>高<rt>たか</rt></ruby>い

Tall / High

<ruby>低<rt>ひく</rt></ruby>い

Short / low

<ruby>暑<rt>あつ</rt></ruby>い

Hot (weather)

<ruby>寒<rt>さむ</rt></ruby>い

Cold (weather)

<ruby>熱<rt>あつ</rt></ruby>い

Hot (to the touch)

<ruby>冷<rt>つめ</rt></ruby>たい

Cold (to the touch)

<ruby>広<rt>ひろ</rt></ruby>い

Wide

<ruby>狭<rt>せま</rt></ruby>い

Narrow

<ruby>厚<rt>あつ</rt></ruby>い

Thick

<ruby>薄<rt>うす</rt></ruby>い

Thin

かん たん
簡単
Easy

むずか
難しい
Difficult

なが
長い
Long

みじか
短い
Short

ふと
太い
Fat / Thick

ほそ
細い
Slim / Thin

おも
重い
Heavy

かる
軽い
Light

あたら
新しい
New

ふる
古い
Old

よ
良い
Good

わる
悪い
Bad

ゆるい
Loose

きつい
Tight

あら
粗い
Coarse

こま
細かい
Fine

はや
速い
Fast

おそ
遅い
Slow

あか
明るい
Bright

くら
暗い
Dark

つよ
強い
Strong

よわ
弱い
Weak

とお
遠い
Far

ちか
近い
Near

やさ
優しい
Kind

きび
厳しい
Strict

しず
静か
Quiet

うるさい
Noisy

き れい
綺麗
Clean / Beautiful

きたな
汚い
Dirty

は で
派手
Flashy

じ み
地味
Plain

じょうず
上手
Good at

へた
下手
Bad at

す
好き
Like

きら
嫌い
Dislike

はや
早い
Early

おそ
遅い
Late

こ
濃い
Dark

うす
薄い
Light

あんぜん
安全
Safe

きけん
危険
Danger

かた
硬い
Hard

やわらかい
Soft

ただ
正しい
Correct

まちが
間違い
Wrong

べんり
便利
Convenient

ふべん
不便
Inconvenience

Onomatopoeia

ワンワン
Bow-wow

ニャーニャー
Meow

メーメー
Baa

ガオー
Roar

コケコッコー
Cluck

モーモー
Moo

ゲロゲロ
Croak

ヒヒーン
Neigh

チューチュー
Squeak

ブーブー
Oink

ホーホー
Hoot

ウッキッキー
Screech

ブーン
Buzz

ガーガー
Quack

コンコン
@@@

カーカー
Caw caw

チュンチュン
Tweet

ワオーン
Awoo

シュー
Hiss

パオーン
Toot

もちもち
Chewy, doughy

ふわふわ
Fluffy, airy

サクサク
Light crispy
(not moist or juicy)

ネバネバ
Slimy / Stringy

ぷるぷる
Jiggly

カリカリ
Crunchy

ピリピリ
Spicy

つるつる
Smooth / Slippery

シュワシュワ
Fizzy / Bubbly

ぷりぷり
Plump / Springy

ホクホク
Fluffy and warm

トロトロ
Long stretching /
sticky / melty

ドキドキ
The rapid heartbeat caused by happiness, fear, surprise

キラキラ
Sparkling / Twinkling

イライラ
Irritable feeling

ペコペコ
Hungry / Starving

ニコニコ
Smiling cheerfully

ワクワク
Excited from anticipation or happiness

ピカピカ
Shiny / Glittering

ペラペラ
To speak foreign language fluently

ザーザー
Heavy rain falling

ヒューヒュー
Strong wind

ムシムシ
Humid and hot

メロメロ
Madly in love

グーグー
To sleep deeply

ウトウト
To start to fall asleep

びしょびしょ
Soggy / Soaked

コンコン
Knocking

Question

What?

なに
何
What

When?

いつ
When

どこ
Where

HOW?

どう
How

Why?

どうして
Why

だれ
誰
Who

どんな
What kind of

なんじ
何時
What time

HOW much?

どのくらい
How much (amount)

HOW MANY?

いくつ
How many, old

Which?

どれ
Which one

With who?

だれ
誰と
With who

いくら
How much (cost/price)

Which one ?

どっち
Which one (of the two)

だれ
誰の
Whose

なぜ
何故
Why (formal)

Counters

ひき / びき / びき
匹
Small animals

ほん / ぽん / ぼん
本
Long, thin objects

だい
台
Machines, Vehicles

はい / ぱい / ばい
杯
Drinks cupfuls, bowlfuls

さつ
冊
Bound objects

にん / り
人
People

とう
頭
Large animals

わ
羽
Birds, Rabbits

まい
枚
Layers, papers, thin, flat objects

こ
個
Small objects

ちゃく
着
Clothes

そく
足
Pairs of shoes, socks

ふん / ぷん
分
Minutes

ねん
年
Years

じ
時
O'clock

えん
円
Yen

かい / がい
階
Building floors

さい
歳
Age

つ
Almost all up to 10

けん
軒
Houses, buildings, shops

にち / か
日
Days

かい
回
Number of times

がつ / つき
月
Number of Months

きょく
曲
Songs, music

き
切れ
Sliced piece of foods

つう
通
Letters, E-mail

ご
語
Words

ぴん / しな
品
Dishes of food

しゅう
週
Weeks

ど
度
Degrees, number of times something happens

かく
画
Kanji Strokes

かん
貫
Sushi

かん
館
Art museums, library

じょう
錠
Tablet medicine

せき
隻
Big Ships

ぜん
膳
Chopsticks

つぼ
坪
Unit of land size

ばん
番
Rank, numbers, turns

はく / ぱく
泊
Number of overnights

さら
皿
Plates of food

ROMAJI

A	I	U	E	O
あ ア	い イ	う ウ	え エ	お オ
Ka	**Ki**	**Ku**	**Ke**	**Ko**
か カ	き キ	く ク	け ケ	こ コ
Sa	**Shi**	**Su**	**Se**	**So**
さ サ	し シ	す ス	せ セ	そ ソ
Ta	**Chi**	**Tsu**	**Te**	**To**
た タ	ち チ	つ ツ	て テ	と ト
Na	**Ni**	**Nu**	**Ne**	**No**
な ナ	に ニ	ぬ ヌ	ね ネ	の ノ
Ha	**Hi**	**Fu**	**He**	**Ho**
は ハ	ひ ヒ	ふ フ	へ ヘ	ほ ホ
Ma	**Mi**	**Mu**	**Me**	**Mo**
ま マ	み ミ	む ム	め メ	も モ
Ya		**Yu**		**Yo**
や ヤ		ゆ ユ		よ ヨ
Ra	**Ri**	**Ru**	**Re**	**Ro**
ら ラ	り リ	る ル	れ レ	ろ ロ
Wa		**O**		**N**
わ ワ		を ヲ		ん ン

Ga	**Gi**	**GU**	**Ge**	**Go**
が ガ	ぎ ギ	ぐ グ	げ ゲ	ご ゴ
Za	**Ji**	**Zu**	**Ze**	**Zo**
ざ ザ	じ ジ	ず ズ	ぜ ゼ	ぞ ゾ
Da	**Ji**	**Zu**	**De**	**Do**
だ ダ	ぢ ヂ	づ ヅ	で デ	ど ド
Ba	**Bi**	**Bu**	**Be**	**Bo**
ば バ	び ビ	ぶ ブ	べ ベ	ぼ ボ
Pa	**Pi**	**Pu**	**Pe**	**Po**
ぱ パ	ぴ ピ	ぷ プ	ぺ ペ	ぽ ポ

Kya	**Kyu**	**Kyo**	**Gya**	**Gyu**	**Gyo**
きゃ キャ	きゅ キュ	きょ キョ	ぎゃ ギャ	ぎゅ ギュ	ぎょ ギョ
Sha	**Shu**	**Sho**	**Ja**	**Ju**	**Jo**
しゃ シャ	しゅ シュ	しょ ショ	じゃ ジャ	じゅ ジュ	じょ ジョ
Cha	**Chu**	**Cho**	**Ja**	**Ju**	**Jo**
ちゃ チャ	ちゅ チュ	ちょ チョ	ぢゃ ヂャ	ぢゅ ヂュ	ぢょ ヂョ
Nya	**Nyu**	**Nyo**	**Hya**	**Hyu**	**Hyo**
にゃ ニャ	にゅ ニュ	にょ ニョ	ひゃ ヒャ	ひゅ ヒュ	ひょ ヒョ
Bya	**Byu**	**Byo**	**Pya**	**Pyu**	**Pyo**
びゃ ビャ	びゅ ビュ	びょ ビョ	ぴゃ ピャ	ぴゅ ピュ	ぴょ ピョ
Mya	**Myu**	**Myo**	**Rya**	**Ryu**	**Ryo**
みゃ ミャ	みゅ ミュ	みょ ミョ	りゃ リャ	りゅ リュ	りょ リョ

Thank you

Thank you for choosing us!

If you found the book helpful or enjoyable,
we would be grateful if you could take a moment
to leave a review.
Your feedback means a lot to us and will help others
discover the book.

ありがとうございます

Made in United States
North Haven, CT
14 June 2025

69813569R00089